the footsteps of Christ

The Journey to the Cross and beyond

VITA ET PAX

THE BENEDICTINE NUNS OF TURVEY ABBEY

MEDITATIONS BY MAUREEN PAMPHILON, OBLATE

MCCRIMMONS
Great Wakering   Essex   England

First published in Great Britain in 1996 by
MCCRIMMON PUBLISHING CO LTD
10-12 High Street, Great Wakering, Essex SS3 0EQ
Tel: (01702) 218956 Fax: (01702) 216082

ISBN 0 85597 559 8

Illustrations have been taken from original oil paintings
of the Stations of the Cross by The Benedictine Nuns
of Turvey Abbey

ACKNOWLEDGEMENTS
The scripture texts have been taken from *The Jerusalem Bible*
© 1966, 1967 & 1968 Darton, Longman & Todd Ltd
and Doubleday & Company, Inc. Used with permission.

Cover design: The Benedictine Nuns of Turvey Abbey

Typeset by McCrimmons: numerals in 72pt Post Antiqua, Headings in 14/18pt Trajan and
main text in 11/13pt Walbaum.

Reprographics by Anagram Litho Ltd, Southend-on-sea, Essex
Printed by Gallpen Press Ltd, Norwich, Norfolk

FOREWORD

These inspired illustrations of Christ's journey to the Cross and beyond are presented to us through colour and symbol. In this book the artist has sought to describe her inspiration for each painting with scripture references, which have been combined with meditations and prayers by Maureen Pamphilon, an oblate of the Turvey community.

Extremely rich in colour the paintings trace Christ's journey to the cross, from Peter's sad denial of his Master and Jesus' willing acceptance of his cross to the crucifixion and entombment, ending with the joy and hope of the resurrection. They offer a vivid feeling of increasing darkness as Christ journeys towards the Cross and the fulfilment of his destiny. From the sombre, dark and beautiful presentation of the entombment we meet Christ risen in glory: darkness to light, sorrow to joy, despair to hope, death to resurrection. The image of the risen Lord in station 16 shatters the overwhelming feeling of darkness and doom with its vivacious display of colour sympathetic with the immense joy of the resurrection. Christ is risen!

The journey to the cross is the story of each person's passage from life to death to life; thus from station to station we are led in meditation on the cross in the world today. And we must always remember that death and resurrection do not only occur when we leave this world, but can and do happen in the daily situations of our lives.

JESUS IS CONDEMNED TO DEATH

The eve of the passion: Jesus' hour of darkness has come when

... all are to be scattered, leaving me alone. *JOHN 16:32*

The colours suggest a glow of fire somewhere ...
in the high priest's courtyard
where Peter sits warming himself.
The cock is crowing,
large, red, fierce and raucous.
All Jesus' friends have deserted him.
Threatening fists, accusing fingers,
are his only reward
for his life of healing and teaching.

Yet I am not alone,
because the Father is with me.
JOHN 16:32

'For our sake God made the sinless one into sin, so that
in him we might become the goodness of God.'
2 CORINTHIANS 5:21

We remember the innocent ones condemned today.
Victims of war and violence,
of earthquake, famine and fire.
We remember the unborn.
And those we condemn by word or deed and even
by our silence – our own brothers and sisters
of every race and creed.

Lord, we pray for all who are treated unjustly.

JESUS TAKES UP HIS CROSS

He seems to welcome it; yet all the horrors of the passion come swooping down on him at this moment. He stands, straight and ready.

It was for this very reason that I came to this hour:
Father, glorify your name. JOHN 12:27-28

Jesus lays down his life for the glory of that name,
so that we might live and give glory to God.

In the stream of suffering engulfing him is also the
strength and love of God.

Jesus embraces the Cross
– God embraces him.

If anyone wants to be a follower of mine, let him
renounce himself and take up his cross and follow me.
MARK 8:34

How do we accept the cross in our lives – ill health,
loneliness, failure or fear? Do we embrace them as
Jesus did?

And how do we respond to the suffering in our
world? To major tragedies? Do we unite with the
victims in our prayer placing them in the presence
of God?

Lord we pray for strength to bear our cross, knowing
that it is your cross we are carrying.

JESUS FALLS THE FIRST TIME

Ours were the sufferings he bore,
ours the sorrows he carried.
ISAIAH 53:4; 1 PETER 2:22-24

He was not carrying that one and only Cross.
He was weighed down, crushed by the crosses of all the
world. Whatever we suffer, Jesus is carrying the weight of it.
He suffers with us. There is no human suffering in which
he is not present to redeem it and to turn it into a seed of
resurrection.

The thorns refer to *Genesis 3:17-18*:

> *Accursed be the soil because of you. ...*
> *It shall yield you brambles and thistles ...*

Jesus came face to face with the curse of paradise.

Your sins are forgiven. Get up, ... and walk. MARK 2:5,11

Thus says Jesus when we fall over and over again
through the frailty of our human condition.

Are we aware of our weaknesses?

Do we pray regularly for strength to overcome
them?

We remember those evil régimes and institutions
and the individuals manipulated by them. Help all
those involved to see the error of their ways.

Lord, when we fall help us to rise and walk
once more with you.

JESUS MEETS HIS MOTHER

This station shows an obvious relief from the previous one. Mary's nearness breaks through the nightmare with light and love; the colours reflect this. Mary was the one who was most able to help and strengthen him, while:

> *... the sword pierced her own soul.*   LUKE 2:35

It is the sword in Mary's heart
that now unites Mother and Son,
comforting each other.
Only when we know suffering ourselves,
can we comfort others.

Let what you have said be done to me.   LUKE 1:38

What are Mary's thoughts as she is reunited with her suffering Son? Does she not experience and share the pain of all mothers
whose children suffer through illness
whose children are missing
whose children are parted from them
through national disasters?

Does she not share also the pain of children, who, perhaps, through a misunderstanding or a desire to be free of parental control are cut off from their loved ones?

Lord, we pray that, as on the way of the cross you brought Mary and her Son together, all families may be united once again in a bond of love.

SIMON OF CYRENE

Just as the good thief was given to understand the secret of the kingdom of Jesus, why should not Simon of Cyrene have been given a glimpse of the Kingdom, piercing through his annoyance at having to carry a criminal's cross by the very act of doing so?

Jesus' head is inclined towards Simon's;
Simon seems to be listening; there is communication.
Jesus is revealing to him the secret of the Kingdom,
the universal call of the human race to

... carry each other's burdens and so fulfil the law of Christ.
GALATIANS 6:2

The background figures illustrate this, here and in the next station.

In so far as you did it to the least of these brothers and sisters of mine, you did it to me. MATTHEW 25:40

Simon helps Jesus unwillingly *(Luke 23:26)* to carry the cross; nevertheless he does help.

Do we allow others to help us in times of great difficulty? By such an action we evoke the Christian virtues of mercy and compassion.

Do we go out of our way to help others in time of need?

Lord help us to extend help willingly to our brothers and sisters when their burdens have become too heavy to carry.

VERONICA

Veronica means 'true image'.

This incident is not recorded in the Gospels but it seems likely that the women who followed Jesus did what they could to ease his suffering.

Veronica has provided us with the ancient representations of the face of Christ 'not made by human hands', venerated in the East. She has given us the face of the *fairest of the children of man (Psalm 44 (45):2)* in whose likeness we must grow, the image that must be impressed on our souls so that we may reflect his glory (cf. *2 Corinthians 3:17-18; 4:6*).

> *It is your face, O Lord, that I seek, hide not your face.*
> PSALM 26 (27):8

A longing to see the face of Christ, to know what he really looked like, has inspired countless artists throughout the ages. It is a frightening challenge too: seeing him face to face may be for us the crucial test of whether we really love him – in our neighbour.

We shall be like him because we shall see him as he really is.   1 JOHN 3:2

Veronica wiped the face of Jesus because she saw before her a suffering person, not knowing that he was the Son of God.

When do we have the opportunity to see the suffering Jesus and offer to comfort him? When? It happens every day.

Lord we pray to love others as you have loved us.

JESUS FALLS THE SECOND TIME

Jesus falls because we fall.

*He became like one
of us, so that we may become like him.*
ST GREGORY OF NAZIANZEN

The crosses of the world (cf. Station no. 3) which
burden him, take on a more tragic dimension;
they seem to batter him down, concentrating on
his faltering figure to crush him totally and for good.

The crosses above, the thorns below:

A man of sorrows, and familiar with suffering.
ISAIAH 53:3

*Come to me, all you who labour and are overburdened,
and I will give you rest.* MATTHEW 11:28

What do we do when someone stumbles and falls
again and again? Do we look around us for someone
to blame? If we do then we are stumbling too.

We remember the homeless throughout the world
those who sleep rough in the big cities
many of whom have lost the will to rise up
and carry on.

Lord, be with all of us who stumble and fall as you
did on the road to Calvary and prompt us to help
others to rise and serve you.

THE WOMEN 8 OF JERUSALEM

If men use the green wood like this,
what will happen when it is dry? LUKE 23:31

Jesus is the green wood, his cross the Tree of Life, from which we all draw fruitfulness.

I am the vine,
you are the branches.
Whoever remains in me, with me in him,
bears fruit in plenty. JOHN 15:5

The cross is represented here as bursting with life. The women too are life-bearers, through suffering.

Jesus wept.   JOHN 11:35

We recall how Jesus shed tears at the death of his friend Lazarus.

Most people at some time of their lives are reduced to tears.

May our tears be not shed in self-pity.

May we in such moments rather weep for the sadness and tragedy of another person's life.

Lord we pray that when darkness engulfs us your light will guide us to extend a helping hand to another in distress.

JESUS FALLS THE THIRD TIME

The crosses are larger and heavier still, to the point of
overwhelming Jesus. He is crushed to the ground.

*Oh how Yahweh in his wrath
has brought darkness on the daughter of Zion!
He has flung the glory of Israel
from heaven to the ground.
All who pass your way
clap their hands at your sight;
they whistle and shake their heads
over the daughter of Jerusalem.
'Was this the loveliest of all,
this the joy of the whole world?'
I am a man familiar with misery
under the rod of his anger.
I am the one he has driven and forced to walk
in darkness and without any light.
And now I say, 'My strength is gone,
that hope which came from Yahweh'.*
LAMENTATIONS 2:1,15; 3:1,18

*Lord if you are willing take this cup away from me.
Nevertheless let your will be done not mine.* LUKE 22:42

We can link this fall of Jesus to his agony in the
Garden of Gethsemane. Jesus weighed down by the
evil in the world falls to the ground and cries out to
his heavenly Father for strength to carry on.

What a lesson for us. We remember so many persons
in our material world searching for help in their distress. Lord hear our pleading, our cries of agony, and
give us strength to overcome all evil.

JESUS IS STRIPPED

Grabbing hands, stripping him of everything.
Jesus let them: he emptied himself.
CF. PHILIPPIANS 2:5-11

Hands grab even at the radiance round his head:
they could not strip him of his divinity.

But God raised him high
and gave him the name
which is above all other names.
PHILIPPIANS 2:9

If anyone loves me he will keep my word,
and my Father will love him,
and we shall come to him
and make our home with him.   *JOHN 14:23*

The Lamb of God who takes away the sins of the
world is prepared for sacrifice. His clothing is torn
away from his body. Love is revealed in its starkest
form.

May we strip ourselves of all attachment to the
things of this world in order that our crucified and
risen Lord may dwell fully in us.

Lord we pray that, having emptied ourselves of all
that separates us from you, the love of God may be
revealed in us, as it was in our brother Jesus.

JESUS IS NAILED TO THE CROSS

Jesus said:

Destroy this sanctuary
and in three days I will raise it up.

JOHN 2:19; MATTHEW 26:61

The background shows the temple, which also
stands for a city on the point of being bombed,
as Jesus' body is on the point of being destroyed
by the nails.

Jesus suffers in the agonies of the human race,
until the end of time.

PASCAL

From that day they were determined to kill him.

JOHN 11:53

The body of Jesus, the son of God, is now secured
to the instrument of torture and people's inhumanity
to another is revealed.

But are things any different today?

We reflect on the destruction/persecution of one
race by another, and on the violence of crime today.

And let us never forget our own failure to love our
neighbour as Jesus taught us.

Lord we pray for all those in our world today whose
intention is the destruction of another.

JESUS SPEAKS TO HIS MOTHER

Like station 4, this is an intermezzo of love and peace,
a moment of warmth and communication. Though
full of pain and distress, the focus here is not on the
pierced hands and feet, nor on the bombed city/
temple, but on the loving concern of three people.
Mary, carrying the sword in her heart, knows that
God is love, and so does John (cf. *1 John 4:16*).

A lasting relationship is established between Mary and John,
soon to be filled with the presence of the risen Jesus. John took
her into his home.

Woman, this is your son. ... This is your mother.

JOHN 19:26

These words are the words of a dying man.
No thought for himself but for the two broken-
hearted people who stood by the cross. His mother
Mary and the disciple John who were very dear to
him. By these words he commends his mother not
only to John but to us all.

We think of those who are spending their lives alone
and in hospitals and homes for the elderly.

Lord we pray for a greater concern for the well-
being of the elderly in our society especially those
with no-one to care for them.

JESUS DIES ON THE CROSS

Darkness is closing in,
confusion,
chaos,
despair.

The background shows the bombed-out city, the temple
of Jesus' body throughout the ages.

The figures of the women standing by him,
the soldiers and the people having watched
    the execution,
turn and walk away,
satisfied?
indifferent?

Father into your hands I commend my spirit.

LUKE 23:46

We adore you O Christ and we bless you. Because
by your holy cross you have redeemed the world.

Before the mystery of the death of our Lord Jesus
on the cross we fall silent. Only adoration remains.

We know that, whatever suffering we have to
undergo in this world, we are held in the hands
of God. His cross is ours.

Lord God our Father we thank you.

JESUS IS TAKEN DOWN FROM THE CROSS

It is over.

Silence and darkness envelop Calvary.

Joseph of Arimathea did a courageous thing,
asking for the body of Jesus. He risked being
identified as one of his friends, an accusation
which had caused Peter's fall.

He did not know about the resurrection,
but unwittingly provided the scene for
the events of Easter.

Truly this was the son of God.   MATTHEW 27:54

Thus said one of his executioners – thus said his
disciples on the sea of Galilee when Jesus calmed
the waters. A profession of faith.

We should all have these words on our lips.

Jesus is taken down from the cross. Mary must have
been there, and the women who followed Jesus.
Mary shares the thoughts of all who hold close to
them a loved one who has died.

Lord, take all whom you have called from this world
into your eternal light, your life and your peace.

JESUS IS BURIED

Deeper darkness still.

But in the deepest shadow of death there is a glimmer of the hope of new life, symbolised by the seedling. Jesus had said:

I tell you most solemnly,
unless a wheat grain falls on the ground and dies,
it remains only a single grain;
but if it dies,
it yields a rich harvest.
JOHN 12:24

Easter expectation begins to shine through the Good Friday sadness.

At the place where he had been crucified there was a garden ... they laid Jesus there.   *JOHN 19:41-42*

The torment and agony of the crucifixion is over and Jesus is laid to rest. He is at peace, but his spirit rises and many of those who had fallen asleep are awakened.

Lord we pray that we may face death with the certain knowledge that we will live forever with you in Christ.

The sun had not yet risen, but HE had!

The news seemed to be too good to be true: it was difficult for the women and the disciples to take it in at first. But as Easter Day unfolded, the proof of his living presence became so overwhelming that they were filled with a joy too great to be contained. And this joy, Jesus said, will never be taken away from us (cf. *John 16:22*).

> The background shows the restored Temple, the City, the New Jerusalem, where Jesus has gone to prepare *many mansions* for us *(John 14:2-4)*.
>
> There is the stream of our Baptism, giving joy to the City *(Psalm 45 (46))* and the new life growing on the river's banks *(Revelation 22:2)*.

Let us adore the holy resurrection of Christ
for behold, through the cross joy has come
   into the world.
Let us always bless the Lord.
Let us sing his resurrection
for by enduring for us the pain of the cross
he has crushed death by dying.

ORTHODOX LITURGY
EASTER SUNDAY

Also by the Benedictine Nuns
of Turvey Abbey ...

■ THE FOOTSTEPS OF CHRIST – POSTERS
Set of 16 posters in full colour / size: A2 (23 $^1/_2$" x 16 $^1/_2$")

Ref: FOCP

■ IN THE LIGHT OF CHRIST
A spiritual resource from the Sisters of Turvey

A clip art resource containing approximately 215 black & white
line art images of varying styles, covering the seasons of Lent,
Easter, Pentecost, Advent, Christmas; the Sacraments,
the Gospel, Unity and general use.
Available on computer floppy disk ($3^1/_2$" HD/DD) for PC–DOS or
Apple Mac.

Ref: ILCDOS   ILCMAC
        (PC Dos format / 4 disks)   (Apple Mac format / 4 disks)

For further details, please contact:
McCrimmons
10-12 High Street, Great Wakering, Essex SS3 0EQ
Tel: (01702) 218956 Fax: (01702) 216082
Ansaphone: (01702) 216544
Our Bookshop at All Saints: (01727) 827612